v v v

Writing in Verse

v v v

Ken Makepeace

v v v

Photo by Sharon McCutcheon

Published by Allpoetry

About the Author

I have been writing for a number of years, ever since I took a creative writing class. I've also had a number of short stories published, on the internet and in small press magazines.

Contents

I Remember When

I remember when the flowers
bloomed so bright and the moon
shone at night and the stars
sparkled in delight.

Those days are forever no-
more as I am locked away
inside, with no place to hide.

No place to dwell, making it seem
like hell.

But one day I'll be free to see the
flowers bloom and moon shine,
and one day I know it will be all
mine.

Down By The Old School Yard

Down by the old school yard
That is where we met
You were ten and I was
nine and I knew that you
would be mine, forever I
hoped. But as we got older
we drifted apart, but it all
started down by the old-
school yard.

Sunrise

Sunrise, sunset
Which is best?

The sun rises in the
morning time and,
apart from the rain,
does it shine,
making it feel all
so fine.

As the evening begins
to call, the sun begins
to fall, making the
sun set for the day,
making me feel so light
and gay.

Next morning it rises again,
making it feel so warm
and tender, feeing it on the
skin, knowing it isn't a sin.

How glad this makes me feel,
knowing the sun is so real,
making life magical even
more, and not letting
life become a bore.

This Knife I Hold

This knife I hold in
my hand, where is
it to land? That is
a question I ask
myself.

I can feel the knife
handle held tight,
not looking for a fight,
but to cut into something
not quite so large

With difficulty the blade
pushes in, to the object
not so thin.

Then as it plunges,
out squirts juice so
plenty, and that's the
last time I'll find
peeling an orange
so hard, and one
that is so juicy.

Nights Close In

Nights close in
Winter approaches
Frost bites
snowflakes fall
Lakes freeze
Thaw begins
Nights lighten
Spring appears
Relieving our fears

Survival Is The Name Of The Game

Survival is the name
of the game
But me? I'd rather
seek fame
So forever remember
my name.

Out Of My Life

You have gone out of
my life, missing, not
seen for months,
maybe never to be
seen again.

But my heart lays
empty without you
around, as though
you don't exist, but
maybe tomorrow
you will be there.

If not, I'll carry on with
my life so bare, so empty
because you are not there.

Shallowness Shying Away

I see shallowness shying
away
A pallid face, sad and lonely
with something to fear, but
maybe not to lear.

Like a leper nobody wants
to know, staring into a world
so void, nobody is getting
annoyed.

Loneliness shows in the face
No one is producing an
ace, this is what I am beginning
to see, not so ugly but
confusing to you and me.

A figure so alone, who is going
into the unknown, staring at
cracks that never reappear
Oh my, what a dear.

Evil is what I see, or is it
Good? Don't ask me.

Autumn Leaves

Autumn leaves, heavy
under foot
Horse chestnuts falling
to the ground.

Dark nights creeping in
Street lights all aglow
People rushing to be near
the fire.

This is the autumn I know
so well, cold and bleak and
not so meek.

Now all we need is some
snow to complete this
autumnal show.

The Stars That Come Out At Night

The stars come out at night
The stars shiny and
bright. How they twinkle
and glisten.

The stars that hover, and make
you wander how many constellations
there are. There must be hundreds by
far. You feel like reaching out and picking
one with your hand. Wouldn't that be grand.

The Days So Lonely

The days so lonely, the nights so cold
But maybe it is me just getting old
My knees creak at the joints,
making life hard to get up the stairs.

But who cares? Who would help?
Being left here with no one to talk to
no one to see. All there is around
is just me.

There Was Nothing There

There was nothing there. Nothing to
share. No one to stare or cast doubt
on anything going wrong.

Life was so perfect. It couldn't be
better. Then it happened. The silence
was broken. The quiet days were left
behind.

How much one person could change
things; bringing noise into a noiseless
world and turning it upside down.

Did I ask for a new neighbour?
One who didn't know how to behave?

Then it all went silent again, just like
it used to be. How did that happen?
I moved away; that is how it happened!

It Was Not A Very Bright Thing To Do

It was not a very bright thing to do,
looking for a shoe. Now what is
going to happen, hopping around
on one leg, with only one shoe
What would you do if it were
you? I know what I'd do, I'd be
hopping mad and wouldn't
that be sad!

Haiku

Summer is not here
Not to come yet for a year
Till then coldness nears

The Moon Glows

The moon glows, the stars shine
It is all mine as I wander this
land in search of peace and
solitude.

Not a soul do I see or meet,
walking these deserted
streets. The solitude I seek
is near and everything is
clear as the moon glows
and the stars shine, all
this peace is mine, hopefully
till the end of time.

Stay With Me Till The Sun Rises

Stay with me till the sun rises
Stay with me till the stars begin
to shine. Tell the world that you
are mine and stay with me till the
end of time.

The Music Plays On

The music kept playing
and I kept listening, to the
tune I did not know.

But the music would keep
playing and I couldn't care
Come to think of it, I wouldn't
Dare.

Did You Miss Me?

Did you miss me while I was away?
I didn't hear you say. Didn't know
if you wanted me to stay?
Anyway, now I am back and
this time I'm staying on the
right track.

The Rain Never Stopped

The rain never stopped and all you got
was more than one drop
It just poured and poured until there
was no more. Then sun began to shine,
making it all mine.

As the day went on, the cold began to near,
Oh, dear, what was I meant to do?
Go home and get warm, stay by the fire
till dawn? But all I could do was yawn.

When dawn came, so did more rain,
So that was it, no more going out. I
Was going to stay in, wouldn't that
Be a sin? But it was better than getting
wet. So that's what I was going to
do, stay in bed till there was one
drop no more.

The Children Of The Revolution

We are the children of the revolution
Don't believe in devolution
Never heard of evolution
Probably because we are the
children of the revolution.

These Moments

These moments may not last
forever, but every second is
so precious and never will be
forgotten, not by me, you, or
anyone.

Why Do I Think About Tomorrow

Why do I think about tomorrow,
with all its sorrow. Not caring about
today, 'cos it is going its own way
And yesterday has gone, never
to come again.

All I want to be left with is memories
Memories of time. Memories that are
all mine.

But there is no going back. Only
forward is the way to go and
remembering all I know, leaving
the world all aglow, and everything
else is left for show.

I'm so restless I cannot sleep

I'm so restless I cannot sleep.
Maybe my thinking is far too
deep.

What do I do for a good night's
sleep? I've even tried counting
sheep.

By the time I drop off, it will
be time to get up.

I could try sleeping in a shoe,
but I'd be too frightened of
catching the flu.

All This Nonsense Doesn't Rhyme

All this nonsense doesn't rhyme
I don't even have the time to
write the line that suits, and I'm
beginning to think I couldn't
care a hoot.

When I finally think I've found
a line, it doesn't seem to want to
fit, making me feel like doing a
moonlight-flit. But carry on I must,
even though I feel like turning into
dust.

.

Sitting In The Park

Sitting in the park, never waiting
for the dark. Never sitting there
for a lark.

There I sat all alone. I didn't even
have my phone, well you wouldn't
if you wanted to be on your own.

I sat there till it was time to go
home, where I stayed all
alone. Should have remained in
the park. I'd have never even
noticed the dark.

Waking Up To Snow On The Ground

Waking up to snow on the ground
So cold to be around. Slipping and
sliding not much fun, but still I'm able
to see the sun.

The cold air making it feel so fresh
How long will it all last? Don't
hold your breath. It'll be here today
but gone tomorrow, taking away all
my sorrow.

Maybe it will snow again; we will have
to wait and see, and if it does, more
slipping and sliding, making me
late getting home for my tea.

Time

Time never to stand still
Time to never say you
will, but time is what we
need; to heal wounds,
mend disagreements

Where would we be with-
out time? Where would we
go, what would we show?
Only time would show and
time would know.

The Parcel That Couldn't Be Delivered

You wait in all day for a parcel
that never arrives, then you
get an email, whatever happened
to snail mail?

The parcel couldn't be delivered.
Making me so mad I started to shiver
Oh, why could they not deliver?

All they had to do was press the
buzzer to my apartment.
It doesn't take a genius. Now
my parcel is coming next week,
making it all seem so bleak.

No more orders from them
Hopefully they'll never be heard
from again.

Never Going Away

My troubles and all my woes
make me think about my toes,
bent and crooked like my thoughts
Never going away, never ending,
like a bad dream that lingers
While I feel like this I do not know.

When days are bad they are really
bad and when they are sad they are
often worse, making me want to
hide from a world I can't abide.

All I want to do is take myself away
and never come back till another day.

Where do I go? What do I do? I am
the only one that knows and that is how
the story goes.

So I tell you now and I'll tell you how,
I get on a bus and travel to nowhere,
Where no one exists, just a stream
Not an ordinary stream, just some-
where to sit and dream and let all
my troubles drift away, giving me
time to think.

Now you know how I beat my troubles
and let everything go, so it just goes
to show what everyone should know
Sit by a stream and let everything go.
Trust everything I say because I should
know.

My favourite colour

My favourite colour has to be,
but no promises to you and me
You think it's red? Why would
that be? Red is the colour,
don't you see? it is the
sign of love and that is all
that matters to you and me.

Walking Along The Road

Walking along, then I crossed
over, well, the grass is always
greener on the other side -
that is what they say!

Not Today

Not today, thank you
I'm not feeling too well.

My Life

My life has been amazing I am sure
Being brought up proper wasn't an issue.

School days ruled and so did the music
Not turning up to class and having a laugh.

My teenage years and my first job
On a fair I did work, but sometimes
I was the one to shirk.

Girls there were a few, but who was
counting? One wanted to marry me
but I was doubting.

Now the autumn years of my life
are now here, but I'm not one to shed
a tear, because I'm having too much fun
with my worrying days gone.

When my time comes there'll be no regrets
I have been fortunate to say the least, where-
ever I go. North, West or East.

This Loneliness Inside

This loneliness inside steals
my heart, takes away my soul,
leaving me empty without a
thought. But one day this
will change and I will become
free, able to live my life happily
and carefree to think about just
you and me.

What Can I say?

What can I say? What can I do?
Here I am living my life without
you. Pining away, dreading
every day. But I know you will
return and stop my heart from
burning, taking away all my yearning.

Who You Really Are

Who you really are? I cannot tell
A poet, you come across so good,
It is though you are in the neighbourhood.

Some of yours I have read and do
I look as though I'm in dread?

You think I don't know you, but in
reality that is not true, and your poems,
I know are not true.

Love you talk about and in one
you talk about having a pen
Just in case you want to know,
my name is Ken. What is yours
I do not know, but I know your poems,
the ones I've read. It is a
pleasure to know and hope
all ends well, but just yet it is
too early to tell.

Times Never Change

Times never change, never alters
Day after day this world keeps
on turning, never ending like
a spinning wheel, revolving
like our thoughts.

Time never stands still for one
moment. it pauses for nobody
Just keeps on for eternity.

This colourful Earth, this planet,
carrying on without a care
Never changing for one instant
What a wonderful place to be,
for you, me and everyone

Waves Crashing Against The Shore

Waves crashing against the shore
Gulls hovering for food.

The smell of the ocean not to be
ignored.

The wind blowing a gale, knowing
no boat is in sight, just brightness
from a lighthouse standing alone,
knowing no one is at home.

With darkness now setting in as the
tide begins to recede. Not a night
to be out, with that there's no doubt,
no doubt indeed.

This Is The day That Never Ends

This is the day that never ends
Never begins as time stands still
What a thrill with nothing to do
Nowhere to go and doesn't it show?
Only we will know what will happen
on the day that never ends.

Night Draws Closer

Night draws closer as
rain continues to pour,
which no one can ignore.

Echoes of silence continue
into the night, leaving no one
to fight, no one to fright.

As daybreak comes so does the
sun, hoping everyone will have
fun, until night draws closer again,
hoping life will still be the same,
even for those looking for fame.
This is certainly not another night
for the rain.

These Lonely Days Here Inside

these lonely days here inside,
sending shivers down my spine,
giving me time to reflect on
the life I am living.

The life I am running away from
The truth is never there. What does
anybody care?

These deep feelings that few
can understand. Spending day
after day, hoping the feelings would
go away.

If this day came I would be free, free
from pain and suffering. But the
isolation is the worst. Waiting for
nobody to come. Just these lonely
days inside, making me want to hide,
or to run away without a care, knowing
there is no one there.

Queuing In The Shops Is Not Fun

Queuing in the shops is not
fun. Waiting ages to get through
the checkout, then finding you
have missed an item out
Too late to go back, so it
is best to do without, unless
the item was the present you
were going to buy me, and
what would it have been?

I wanted a yacht or a racing car,
or maybe a jet to take me far. But
what will I finish up with? A plastic
duck I can play with while taking
a bath.

I've got some news for you, I've only
a shower. No bath for a duck, so
what can I do? Take a walk in
the park and find a real one and
feed it some bread, then go home
and take a shower and think about
the world instead.

What Did Anybody Know?

What did anybody know?
What did anybody care?
Just not wanting to be
there. To be left alone
in solitude. The sound
of silence so clear, yet
no one is so near.

To be left to think and
dream. To live in a world
with no team. Just me
alone with my thoughts

And that is how it ought to
be, no one there except
thee.

A Day To Daydream

A day to daydream, no one knows
A day to daydream, no goes
But tomorrow will come and
so will the sun. But what will
tomorrow bring? Will it be none?

A day to daydream, we will be
there. A day to daydream who
will care?

A day to daydream I know where
I'll be, watching out to see who
is following me. Maybe no one,
we will see. Maybe it is you or
it could be me, following a dream
that nobody can see.

Walking By A Stream

Walking by a stream, thinking
about tomorrow, thinking about
my sorrow, the grief I have inside.

The lonely times I've tried to walk away
from, the tears I hide. Will there
be anymore tomorrows from which
I cannot abide? It's all left for me to
decide from which I cannot deny.

But all the pain and suffering will one
day vanish, and I'll be free to live my life.

Still walking past this stream, maybe
things are not so bad
All I have to do is be happy and things
will work out fine. They usually do if they
are given time. And that is one thing I
have got plenty of. The whole of the world
is mine.

The Sun Shining

With the sun shining, it was too hot
to be inside, to hide away just for
the day, but hey, there's a better idea
to get away from it all.

To go for a day out in the park,
where a picnic would be fun,
in the shade away from the sun

Sandwiches you could take with
a filling that would not be fake and
you could even bake a cake, and
some lemonade would be fun,
which you could drink if you decided
to sit in the sun.

And when the day comes to end
you may find you have made a new
friend. What a fun day you had, I can
hear you say. All that from having
a picnic in the park.

What did I know?

What did I know? what did I care?
Was it time to share? But one day
maybe I will meet you there,
who will know? Who will tell?
Maybe I'll just go back into my shell.

Cold And Hungry

Cold and hungry
Nowhere to go
Just living on the
streets with no one
to know.

Just waiting for somebody to
turn up to give me some food,
but I just keep feeling in a
mood.

Then someone arrives and
I am not alone, All I want now
is someone to give me a home.

Time Wouldn't Stand Still

Time wouldn't stand still for
those who didn't know,
or didn't even want to be there.

But did they care or even
notice? I doubt it. But let
them stare, while we carry
on till a time there will be
none.

Standing The Test Of Time

Standing the test of time,
oh to be mine. How I wonder
through this land, making
life so grand. I was thinking
of starting a band, but I kept
things in hand to stand the
test of time.

Time passes slowly

Time passes slowly,
so slow it is hard to believe.
But where would we be
without time?

Suspended in animation, waiting
for nothing to happen, with nowhere
to go and nothing to show.

But time leads us on. Takes us
places we want to go. Heals
wounds that are long overdue
and helps us fulfil dreams we
have, and desires too, So don't
complain about time passing
slowly, use it to your gain and
realize things will never be
the same.

The Tears I Want To Hide

The tears I want to hide, the
tears I want to share. Does anybody
care? But I think you do, and I do too,
caring about each other, not looking
for another.

So that is how we will stay, together
forever in perfect harmony.

Why Do People Hurry?

Why do people hurry? Why do people
worry? I do not know, I do not care.
I just want to walk away, hoping for
a brand new day. A fresh start, away
from the past, hoping it would last.

Getting away from it all is the only
way to be, maybe just for you and
me.

So that is what we will do, runaway
and leave everything behind, and
without a care, would they dare?

Let them worry, let them hurry. It
will not bother us. We will be
past caring, past sharing, away
from it all, not letting us the ones
to fall, leaving them behind. Don't
worry, we won't mind.

There Was Nowhere To Go

There was nowhere to go,
nothing to do. It was like
sitting in a shoe. No room
to move. No room to groove.

What could you do? Stay
at home and not answer
the phone and just sit
there all alone.

But you'd soon get bored
and think, oh Lord what
am I to do? What could
you do? What could you
say? Nothing but just
sit there all day.

When Times Are Trying

When times are trying and there
is nowhere to go, and nothing to know
All you can do is switch on the radio
and let yourself go.

Listen to the hits of yesterday, listen
to them now. All the tunes from the
70s and let your mind allow.

Or you could listen to the 60s, bringing
back the good times, for all we know.

Just sit back and relax and listen to the
show.

Another Day Beckons

Another day beckons. What does it
hold? Maybe many mysteries that
are ready to be told.

Whatever the day holds we are to
be grateful for what we receive
And one thing is for sure, we don't want
anyone to deceive, or play the game
unfair. So treat everyone with respect,
then life will turn out fair.

What Are People Trying To Say?

What are people trying to say?
Maybe I'm not listening and that
is my way. Maybe I am just saving
it for another day.

Whatever people might say, whatever
people might do, it is entirely up to whether you
take them seriously.

Personally I would ignore them and
not give them the time of day, but, hey
that is for me to decide, even if I wanted
to hide. One thing that I can honestly say
is that I've never lied, nor ever told an untruth
So I can say my conscience is clear and
believe me my friend, that is very dear.

Nights Feel Lonely

Nights feel lonely. Nights
feel cold; but only when you
are not by my side.

Which is so often these days
that I cannot stand why you
don't want to be around.

Whatever I did. Whatever I said
I do not know. But my feelings are
always on show.

Maybe one day you'll realize that
I am not messing you around and
we can forget all are troubles and
all will be sound.

Thinking Of What To Write

Thinking of what to write is never
easy, but thinking about you is.

The beauty you show makes
me wanting to know.

Looking into your eyes makes
me realize how radiant you are,
like a star shining so bright, never
needing the light.

In my mind you will always be.
There'll never be another for me,
even if I live till I'm a hundred
and three.

Sometime Things Are Better Left Unsaid

Sometimes things are best left unsaid,
'specially before you go to bed.

In the morning things seem brighter,
and a lot lighter.

A night's sleep can help with your problems
Gives your mind time to recharge its batteries
and stops you from saying things you'd
otherwise regret.

So start the day with a clear mind and leave
the others behind. But no doubt they'll
think you are being unkind. Just walk
away and never mind.

There Were Times When I Felt Troubled

There were times when I felt
troubled. There were times when
I felt lonely, But only because you
were not around, making everything
not so sound.

Then you returned and my life
changed, to being happy, smiling
my days through, and all because
of you.

You are my sweetness and light and
and there is never any need for a fight.
And I feel so good that I could love
you for more than one night.

A lifetime being more like, bringing
days of sunshine, making every day fine
and definitely till the end of time,

They Stood There Watching

They stood there watching - but why?
What was happening? No one wanted
to tell. For all they knew they could go
to hell.

But they still stood there. Was time
standing still? Were they too busy
to walk up that hill?

We'll never know. We will never
care as they stood just watching
there.

Winter Is Upon Us

Winter is upon us and snow
is on the ground? But why
does it have to be so cold?
Does it mean I'm getting old?

If the snow would go away and it
would be warm again someday,
would my old age go away?

If it did I'd feel young and wouldn't
wait for it to want to snow. But here
I am getting confused and not knowing
what to do. So old age must
be coming and there is nothing I
can do. So just hope one day that
it doesn't happen to you

Tomorrow never comes

Tomorrow never comes
Today never ends. But
what about yesterday?

Was that the day you went
away? The day I wanted you
to stay?

I know you'll never say or
ever enter my life again,
but maybe you'll change
your mind. Who will ever
know? Maybe no one,
especially if tomorrow never
comes and today never ends.

So we will leave it at that, knowing
it'll never last, and all there is to do
now is live in the past.

Hoping Tomorrow Won't Be Full Of

Sorrow

Hoping tomorrow won't be full of sorrow,
unlike today, feeling unhappy in every way.

The feeling of hopelessness taking a grip
I couldn't even be bothered to go out for a trip.

But I know one day that things will change,
making me not wanting to get in a rage.

Maybe all this is down to my age, or
maybe is because I'm not the centre
of the stage.

Will You Love Me For A Reason

Will you love for a reason?
Will you love me till the end
of the season?

Will you love me till there's no
tomorrow? Will you love me till
there's no sorrow?

If you do, I hope it is till the end
of time, then you will be all mine.

Too Many Broken Hearts

Too many broken hearts,
too many crosses to bear.
But would that stop you
wanting to be around?
Or not wanting to care? Or
would you say dare? All I
know is, I need you to be
there.

The Pain Never Goes Away

The pain never goes away
My heart aches like there
is no tomorrow. Is there
any cure for this sorrow,
deep down inside, with
no peace from my mind?

The days since you left me
behind, knowing there'd
be no cure - that you knew
for sure.

But now you cannot lure me to
your way thinking. I'd rather let
my heart sink down below the
surface to a place far away, and
know for sure, you'll never see
that day.

He Was The Greatest

He was the greatest of them all
He was the rise and fall.

Ziggy Stardust and the men
from Mars.

Space Oddity I loved, and
and 'Ground control to Major
Tom' was an amazing line.

Listen to Bowie if you want
an incredible time, and then
you'll know everything is just
fine.

The countryside is so appealing

The countryside is so appealing
and so calm - a place where no-
one can come to harm.

You can visit any time you want.

You'll also love the peace and
quiet, knowing there'll never be
a riot!

How I Love You

How I love you to this day, and
these are the words I want to say -

I miss you every moment, every
second that passes, like ships in
the night, never missing the light.

I love you so bright, but now I must
wish you goodnight , for tomorrow
there will be no sorrow with thoughts
of you in my mind, and nobody could
say that love is unkind.

Held The Ace

Leather Face held the ace
Always feared, never straight
Never late for a crime he
committed, even if he didn't
admit it.

Now here he stood in a line-up,
showing no remorse for a crime
he didn't commit, or that is what he
said. He told the police he was in
bed. Hard to believe since they
found him in a bank

He told them he was sleep-walking
Didn't even realize he was threatening
the teller. Just thought he was another
fella.

The police told him to tell his story
to the judge. But guess what?
He wouldn't budge.

But the judge wasn't impressed
Gave him thirty years, which
drove Leather Face to tears.

Now here he was languishing
behind bars, whishing he had
been sent to Mars!

since Leather Face had
been given his fate, he now
only has a prison warder for
a date.

Angel Standing In The Dark

Angel standing in the dark.
Is it you I hear?

You want to be mine till
there is time no more,
waiting forever, hoping
I will call your name,
never wanting to sound
so vain.

I know one day you will
drive me insane with desire,
because you know how to
light my fire.

With flames so intense,
you'll be asking me where is
my sense? I lost it when
I found you begging for my
body forever more, but then I
changed my mind and headed
toward the door!

I Dream Of Jeannie

I dream of Jeannie so light and so fair
I dream of Jeannie, I hope she will be
there to make all wishes come true
for me and for you. So I dream of Jeannie
to save the day and make all our dreams
come our way.

Printed in Great Britain
by Amazon

17622585R00051